Adam is in bed, sleeping. He is having a good dream . . .

He's fast. He's strong. 'Good work, James Bond!'

But Adam is not James Bond – it is only a dream. Adam works in a bank, and it is not very interesting. He doesn't like his job and he doesn't like Mr Smith, his boss. Adam is not happy – he wants a more exciting life.

It is Monday morning. Adam is walking to work and he meets Mrs B. 'Do something different today,' she says. Adam starts to walk again. He stops and waits at the side of the road. He usually goes left next, but then he remembers Mrs B's words. So he goes right . . .

What happens next? Does his life change? Can dreams come true?

OXFORD BOOKWORMS LIBRARY

Crime & Mystery

Give us the Money

Starter (250 headwords)

MAEVE CLARKE

Give us the Money

Illustrated by
Axel Rator

OXFORD UNIVERSITY PRESS

OXFORD
UNIVERSITY PRESS

Great Clarendon Street, Oxford OX2 6DP

Oxford University Press is a department of the University of Oxford.
It furthers the University's objective of excellence in research, scholarship,
and education by publishing worldwide in

Oxford New York

Auckland Cape Town Dar es Salaam Hong Kong Karachi
Kuala Lumpur Madrid Melbourne Mexico City Nairobi
New Delhi Shanghai Taipei Toronto

With offices in

Argentina Austria Brazil Chile Czech Republic France Greece
Guatemala Hungary Italy Japan Poland Portugal Singapore
South Korea Switzerland Thailand Turkey Ukraine Vietnam

OXFORD and OXFORD ENGLISH are registered trade marks of
Oxford University Press in the UK and in certain other countries

ISBN: 978 0 19 423413 9

Printed in China

Word count (main text): 690

For more information on the Oxford Bookworms Library, visit
www.oup.com/bookworms

This book is printed on paper from certified and well-managed sources.

CONTENTS

GLOSSARY

boring not interesting

boss the person who tells you what to do at work

cut a film director shouts this to stop the film

film a story that you watch on television or at the cinema

film set the place where you make a film

greedy when you want too much money or food

holiday when you have a rest from work or school

hurt to feel pain; if you shut your finger in a door, your finger hurts

real something that is true or something you can touch

robber a person who takes something that is not his or hers, especially from a bank.

same not different

show when you use your hand to indicate something

thief another word for robber

voice the noise you make when you speak

Give us the Money

ACTIVITIES

ACTIVITIES

Before Reading

1 **Look at the front and back cover of the book. Choose the correct endings.**

1 Adam . . .
a ☐ is a secret agent.
b ☐ works in a bank.
c ☐ is an actor.

2 The beautiful young woman is . . .
a ☐ an actor.
b ☐ a thief.
c ☐ an English teacher.

3 This is . . .
a ☐ a romantic story.
b ☐ an exciting story.
c ☐ a sad story.

ACTIVITIES

While Reading

1 **Read pages 1–3, then answer these questions.**

   1 What does Adam want to be?
   2 What time of day is it?
   3 Why is Adam bored with his job?
   4 What does Mrs B. say to Adam?

2 **Read pages 4–5.**
   Are these sentences true (T) or false (F)?

		T	F
1	Adam does something different today.	☐	☐
2	Some men take a woman's rucksack.	☐	☐
3	The woman asks Adam for help.	☐	☐
4	The men run after Adam and the women.	☐	☐

3 **Before you read pages 6–9,**
   can you guess what happens next?

		YES	NO
1	The woman, Serena, thanks Adam for his help.	☐	☐
2	The police arrest the thieves.	☐	☐
3	The thieves hurt somebody.	☐	☐
4	Serena and Adam fall in love.	☐	☐

4 Read pages 10–13, then answer these questions.

1 How do Adam and Serena get away?
2 What is Serena's idea?
3 Why is the director happy?

5 Read pages 14–18, then answer these questions.

1 Why does Serena's car stop?
2 What do the thieves want?
3 What does Adam do?
4 Adam knows one of the thieves. Who is he?

6 Read pages 19–21, then answer these questions.

1 Who are the 'police'?
2 What does Serena take from Adam?
3 What does she do with it?
4 What do they tie Mr Smith with?

7 Read pages 22–24. Who says these sentences?

1 'I *am* late for work!'
2 'You're three hours late.'
3 'Say "please".'
4 'I want you to be a bank robber.'

ACTIVITIES

After Reading

1 Use these words to complete the summary of the story.

arrest gun boss bank film thieves take angry afraid

Adam wants to be James Bond. He sees two men _____ a
woman's bag and tries to help. The men are _____. They
are very _____ when they see that they have got the
wrong bag. They follow Serena and Adam. Adam is very
_____ but Serena is not. Serena uses a water _____ to stop
one of the thieves. When the thief speaks, Adam
understands that the thief is his _____. The police _____
the thieves. Serena and Adam take the money to the _____
and the film director asks Adam to be in his _____ as a
bank robber!

2 Write a short description of Serena.

....
....
....
....
....

3 **Read the clues below
and complete the crossword.**

ACROSS

1 The man or woman who performs in a film.
5 Something you carry with you.
   You can speak to people with it.
8 A public garden.
9 The opposite of interesting.
10 You can read about what is happening in the world.

DOWN

2 The person who takes something which is not his.
3 A bag you wear on your back.
4 Another word for picture or movie.
6 A place where you can put or get money.
7 When you take a rest from school or work, often in
   another country.

ABOUT THE AUTHOR

Maeve Clarke is an experienced teacher and examiner of English as a Foreign Language. She has worked in England, Spain, and Italy. She now lives in Birmingham and works with students from all over Europe, in Birmingham's European Summer University.

She wrote *Give us the Money* because she wanted to write a story about something exciting happening on a boring Monday. Maeve has also written a novel, *What Goes Round*, and a short story *Letters A Yard*, (part of the award-winning collection, *Whispers in the Walls*).

OXFORD BOOKWORMS LIBRARY

Classics • Crime & Mystery • Factfiles • Fantasy & Horror
Human Interest • Playscripts • Thriller & Adventure
True Stories • World Stories

The OXFORD BOOKWORMS LIBRARY provides enjoyable reading in English, with a wide range of classic and modern fiction, non-fiction, and plays. It includes original and adapted texts in seven carefully graded language stages, which take learners from beginner to advanced level. An overview is given on the next pages.

All Stage 1 titles are available as audio recordings, as well as over eighty other titles from Starter to Stage 6. All Starters and many titles at Stages 1 to 4 are specially recommended for younger learners. Every Bookworm is illustrated, and Starters and Factfiles have full-colour illustrations.

The OXFORD BOOKWORMS LIBRARY also offers extensive support. Each book contains an introduction to the story, notes about the author, a glossary, and activities. Additional resources include tests and worksheets, and answers for these and for the activities in the books. There is advice on running a class library, using audio recordings, and the many ways of using Oxford Bookworms in reading programmes. Resource materials are available on the website <www.oup.com/bookworms>.

The *Oxford Bookworms Collection* is a series for advanced learners. It consists of volumes of short stories by well-known authors, both classic and modern. Texts are not abridged or adapted in any way, but carefully selected to be accessible to the advanced student.

You can find details and a full list of titles in the *Oxford Bookworms Library Catalogue* and *Oxford English Language Teaching Catalogues*, and on the website <www.oup.com/bookworms>.

THE OXFORD BOOKWORMS LIBRARY
GRADING AND SAMPLE EXTRACTS

STARTER • 250 HEADWORDS

present simple – present continuous – imperative –
can/cannot, must – *going to* (future) – simple gerunds ...

Her phone is ringing – but where is it?

Sally gets out of bed and looks in her bag. No phone. She looks under the bed. No phone. Then she looks behind the door. There is her phone. Sally picks up her phone and answers it. *Sally's Phone*

STAGE 1 • 400 HEADWORDS

... past simple – coordination with *and*, *but*, *or* –
subordination with *before*, *after*, *when*, *because*, *so* ...

I knew him in Persia. He was a famous builder and I worked with him there. For a time I was his friend, but not for long. When he came to Paris, I came after him – I wanted to watch him. He was a very clever, very dangerous man. *The Phantom of the Opera*

STAGE 2 • 700 HEADWORDS

... present perfect – *will* (future) – *(don't) have to*, *must not*, *could* –
comparison of adjectives – simple *if* clauses – past continuous –
tag questions – *ask/tell* + infinitive ...

While I was writing these words in my diary, I decided what to do. I must try to escape. I shall try to get down the wall outside. The window is high above the ground, but I have to try. I shall take some of the gold with me – if I escape, perhaps it will be helpful later. *Dracula*

STAGE 3 • 1000 HEADWORDS
... should, may – present perfect continuous – *used to* – past perfect –
causative – relative clauses – indirect statements ...

Of course, it was most important that no one should see
Colin, Mary, or Dickon entering the secret garden. So Colin
gave orders to the gardeners that they must all keep away
from that part of the garden in future. ***The Secret Garden***

STAGE 4 • 1400 HEADWORDS
... past perfect continuous – passive (simple forms) –
would conditional clauses – indirect questions –
relatives with *where/when* – gerunds after prepositions/phrases ...

I was glad. Now Hyde could not show his face to the world
again. If he did, every honest man in London would be proud
to report him to the police. ***Dr Jekyll and Mr Hyde***

STAGE 5 • 1800 HEADWORDS
... future continuous – future perfect –
passive (modals, continuous forms) –
would have conditional clauses – modals + perfect infinitive ...

If he had spoken Estella's name, I would have hit him. I was so
angry with him, and so depressed about my future, that I could
not eat the breakfast. Instead I went straight to the old house.
Great Expectations

STAGE 6 • 2500 HEADWORDS
... passive (infinitives, gerunds) – advanced modal meanings –
clauses of concession, condition

When I stepped up to the piano, I was confident. It was as if I
knew that the prodigy side of me really did exist. And when I
started to play, I was so caught up in how lovely I looked that
I didn't worry how I would sound. ***The Joy Luck Club***

BOOKWORMS · CRIME & MYSTERY · STARTER

Girl on a Motorcycle

JOHN ESCOTT

'Give me the money,' says the robber to the Los Angeles security guard. The guard looks at the gun and hands over the money. The robber has long blond hair and rides a motorcycle – and a girl with long blond hair arrives at Kenny's motel – on a motorcycle. Is she the robber?

BOOKWORMS · CRIME & MYSTERY · STARTER

Oranges in the Snow

PHILLIP BURROWS AND MARK FOSTER

'Everything's ready now. We can do the experiment,' says your assistant Joe.

You are the famous scientist Mary Durie working in a laboratory in Alaska. When you discover something very new and valuable, other people want to try to steal your idea – can you stop them before they escape?

BOOKWORMS · THRILLER & ADVENTURE · STARTER

Drive into Danger

ROSEMARY BORDER

'I can drive a truck,' says Kim on her first day at work in the office. When Kim's passenger Andy finds something strange under the truck things get dangerous – very dangerous.

BOOKWORMS · CLASSICS · STARTER

The Ransom of Red Chief

O. HENRY

Retold by Paul Shipton

Bill and Sam arrive in the small American town of Summit with only two hundred dollars, but they need more and Sam has an idea for making a lot of money. When things start to go very wrong, both men soon regret their visit – and the idea.

BOOKWORMS · CRIME & MYSTERY · STAGE 1

Love or Money?

ROWENA AKINYEMI

It is Molly Clarkson's fiftieth birthday. She is having a party. She is rich, but she is having a small party – only four people. Four people, however, who all need the same thing: they need her money. She will not give them the money, so they are waiting for her to die. And there are other people who are also waiting for her to die.

But one person can't wait. And so, on her fiftieth birthday, Molly Clarkson is going to die.

BOOKWORMS · CRIME & MYSTERY · STAGE 1

Sister Love and Other Crime Stories

JOHN ESCOTT

Some sisters are good friends, some are not. Sometimes there is more hate in a family than there is love. Karin is beautiful and has lots of men friends, but she can be very unkind to her sister Marcia. Perhaps when they were small, there was love between them, but that was a long time ago.

They say that everybody has one crime in them. Perhaps they only take an umbrella that does not belong to them. Perhaps they steal from a shop, perhaps they get angry and hit someone, perhaps they kill . . .